Contents

**Being
Gemini**

Being
Gemini
Marilyn Longstaff

Smokestack Books
School Farm
Nether Silton
Thirsk
North Yorkshire
YO7 2JZ

e-mail: info@smokestack-books.co.uk
www.smokestack-books.co.uk

Poems copyright
Marilyn Longstaff, 2024,
all rights reserved.

Author photograph
John Longstaff.

Cover image:
details from *Brechtian Gestures: Marilyn*, 2022,
© Fiona Crangle.

Cover image design:
Pat Maycroft

ISBN 9781739473464

Smokestack Books
is represented by
Inpress Ltd.

for my grandchildren
Alba and Oliver

and in memory of
my grandson Joseph

Cluff (after Dürer)

NO, I DON'T THINK THE EFFECTS OF POST
CREATION TRAUMA HAVE WORN OFF YET, EITHER

Gemini

I signed a contract with myself
after my last major falling.
The wayward, brave, foolhardy me,
my passionate, reckless twin,
I wrapped in purple velvet and fuchsia silk,
incarcerated her at the bottom of
my sailor's oak chest at the foot of my
marriage bed, placed blankets on top
for smothering.

In Autumn, she settles a little with the
earlier and earlier drawing of thick curtains.
In Winter, she's dormant and I'm happy
in front of a blazing fire, hibernating.
I never let her out, although in Spring,
when the sap's rising, she rattles the lid and
itches my skin, humming a half-remembered
ditty, an earworm she's planted to make me
restless, scratchy.

The Officer

The Officer
blamed harmful reading
she'd promised to eschew

but he couldn't argue with
the A level English Syllabus.
D.H. Lawrence, *Selected Essays*,

so dull, she reasoned she needed
to read around the subject:
Women in Love, Sons and Lovers,

she read them all – even the one
unbanned in 1960, second hand,
that fell open at certain pages.

He'd managed to keep her from
dangerous films, wicked make-up,
the demon drink,

but if truth be told,
he recognised her sinful nature,
knew it had all started long before.

The Officer's Daughter

First she left God, at 17 – stopped believing.
Then she left home – 'The Quarters' in Darlington –
the rest a gradual slipping,

years of unpicking: rituals, uniform,
ways of seeing stitched into the fabric of her being.
In all her childhood years of moving, she never left:

The Citadel, the congregation, brass bands, tambourines,
Penitent Form, The Platform, the whole shebang
of Victorian military evangelical belonging.

This was her family. She married out.
After nightmare years, she stopped dreaming.
Home is a place she can't go back to.

A note to myself growing up

You know when you were too frit
to get up in the night
in the dark
in the cold
        even though you needed a wee
        and you had to cross your legs
for fear of the witches
who lived under the bed
and the goblins that creaked on the stairs
and the black inside of the outside lav
hiding demons and devils.

And your Mum said, 'don't be daft,
they're not real
they only exist in fairy tales
and we are children of the light,
we're safe in the arms of Jesus.'

Well, she didn't mention
it comes at a price – this certainty,
and the cost is believing,
which is good if you can.

Triptych – Sheer Colour

after Trinity Stained Glass by John McLean
at Norwich Cathedral

It was the light that stopped me.
Perfect midsummer day

and the 5 o'clock sun
at exactly the right angle

to cast orange and red rays
from the *God The Son* window,

all the stone of this north aisle
bathed in blood-warm glow.

In my head, I understand:
the cool blues of *God The Father,*

The Holy Spirit's ethereal yellows,
but they don't reach me –

too lofty and intellectual,
not hot   visceral   sun-burning.

I'll carry on,
tread the fiery coals.

Camino

She always wanted to walk
up and across the Pyrenees, then down
to Santiago de Compostela

> this is no journey
> for the flaxen-haired,
> the pale-skinned –
> boots rubbing, face aches
> from squinting; I wish I'd
> brought more paper hankies

beyond hot on the plains,
icy on the mountains, everything
she packed is heavy and unsuitable

> I haven't cut or washed
> or combed my fine gold hair
> for months; it's knotted, tangled –
> I think something creeping
> has moved in; my deodorant
> ran out weeks ago

looked so inviting in the brochure –
organised for the solitary wayfarer;
challenge yourself, it said

> how I hate all flying insects:
> black flies settle on sweaty
> limbs, sweaty sandwiches
> I am beset by pilgrims –
> their enforced jollity,
> shallow kindnesses

If she were travelling on a spiritual highway,
she could follow her mother's shunned advice,
rise above it

Falletery

I had to escape
my husband's propensity

to preach, his certainty
as crown of creation.

I could be only second best.
Not to mention

the disagreeable rib that
would always come between us.

> A typo, a misprint, that
> master of the Freudian slip

> knew what I wanted,
> saw what I lacked

> that even nakedness was dull
> in the land of pure pleasure.

There was, of course,
nothing to complain about.

How could there be? Just
a shadow of a ghost of a hint

that all was not quite fair.
So it's not surprising, is it

that in all this beauty,
this cloying goodness,

I was a fruit ripe to be picked.

Fractured

She stands by the scrubbed pine table,
her hair bound under a white cloth,
holds to her chest the fractured pot –
the mistress's prized Chinese porcelain.
Her spine curves, her body slumps.
She is heavy with fear.

She doesn't know how she broke it.
She has tamed her careless gene.
All these years of tying it down,
smoothing her fractured edges.
Her mistress is unforgiving –
You're only as good as your last mistake.

Smooth, another word for bland.
She tries to disguise her irritation
but her face is a dead giveaway –
eyebrows join, mouth thins, tilts,
her eyes darken. She must practice
in front of the glass:

never quite white. Dark creases
in the folds of her belly,
liver spots, blue bulging veins,
red-rimmed eyes, silver ring
on her wedding finger.
As others fade, she blooms.

She recalls mountains. Pain slices
across her patella. It's contrary:
worse in better weather.
Grounded in everyday trouble
and trouble ahead, she frets,
frets, waits for the storm.

MCC learns a lesson from cricket

'You can swallow poison and live.'
Vicki Thomas

Amazing how a gift comes to you from left field,
when you're guarding the wicket
                    minding your own business,
somewhere on the crease you have marked
and then made deeper – so deep,
only your eyes can peep above it
if you stand on tiptoe.   Why?

Safe in here – a rut of your own making,
even if the bat isn't yours. You've settled for it.

Then the hard ball comes straight for you,
just as you are taking a sinister glance,
a one-in-a-thousand chance,
hits you right between the eyes,
knocks you for six, knocks you sideways,
knocks you off your guard,
knocks you.

Twin

Her hair – wild blonde curls – bound.
        She hated the tight pinching head-dressing,
scratched at it.
        My hair is straight, fine, dark.

We loved to roll in the deep Persian carpet
        breathe in its dust, in spite of beating
wove fantasies from foreign patterns
        imagined it flying us   Elsewhere.

I was the first-born
        charged with responsibility and control – I failed her.

I haven't seen her since my marriage bed.
        She went to the bad
escaped the tight corsets, breast-board,
                unremitting husband.

Like carved wooden lions, we roared   within.
She would wail, smash crockery,
throw over-ripe apples at the wall.   I am tied
        buttoned, dry-eyed – flutter inside.

Did her untamed heart survive,
        was she cold, stinking, drunken?
I'll lock the door to that room –
              persevere.

Walking with Dot

Sandsend to Whitby, 11 January 2020

Strong wind gusting on our backs:

we bless it, praise it, thank it
for its helpful, firm propulsion.

We feel the sand is blowing
as it rushes past our heels and ankles,

whipping-up like a locust swarm
or snaking like a pale murmuration.

We stride out, talking ten-to-the dozen –
that easy chat of comrades – blind to the

sandstorm stinging the bare red cheeks
of walkers battling in the opposite direction.

We know the tide is coming in, realise
almost all is behind us, recognise inevitability,

but for a moment, we are safe, cushioned,
                                    warm.

Visiting Mum at Christmas

April 2020

On Christmas Eve in 1987,
half way through a bowl of mushroom soup in Debenhams,
                                                    Bournemouth,
I realised I couldn't carry on,

took to my bed that night with flu, didn't get up for 14 days,
apart from lying on the rear seat of the Ford Orion
for the 320 mile journey home to Saltburn.

Another two weeks and a stone lighter.

That Christmas Day, my Mum took umbrage,
'I've been to all this trouble. Surely you can manage a little dinner.'

I think I might be pregnant changed her tune.
She called the doctor out. She had a track record.
Seven months later, the baby boy was fine.

It's Day 12 for my daughter: still no sense of taste or smell,
total exhaustion, a breathy voice. She's lost the cough
and never had the fever. And she's miles away in London.

Missing my Mum, who called the doctor out
on Christmas Day in 1983
when I was first pregnant: excruciating stomach pains

he diagnosed as indigestion.   Come on my Girl
get better soon. You, who were born in Whitby Hospital
at the height of the miners' strike. Come on fighter,

beat the Covid Bastard.

Landlocked Ramble

May 2020

Somewhere ages and ages hence:
Two roads diverged in a wood, and I –
I took the one less travelled by,
And that has made all the difference.
Robert Frost

It's odd but I haven't been somewhere
else, other than here, for ages and ages,
or so it seems; it's less than three months and
I'm fit and well, but this lockdown ages
me; I've hit my seventieth birthday, hence
the existential crisis. I'm not alone. The two
of us have been out every day, pounded the roads,
streets, back lanes. Sometimes we've diverged
from our normal familiar routes, taking in
a blind alley, a cul-de-sac, someone's drive, a
forbidden path; trespassed through a wood
with nettles, on the outskirts, with no exit and
finding ourselves vaulting a high wall that I
had real trouble with, into busy traffic. I
have been the more careful. I always took
a wide berth round other couples, the
plethora of pavement cyclists, that one
sweaty jogger who couldn't care less.

Although confined, my mind has travelled
from the here-and-now to *the sweet by-and-by*
not the *beautiful shore* of the hereafter and
the company of angels, but earthly shores that
seem almost within my grasp, and that hope has
kept me sane. Memories of the sea have made
a sound poem in my heart, everything and all
about it: a whistle, a roar, a gentle shush, the
bass of its varied power, its tenor of difference.

Ouse Water Meadow, York

4 June 2020

I can see clover –
I know what that is –

and some little yellow flowers
I've looked up before.
A multitude of different grasses,
all very long, make a satisfying slap
against my calves.

A few golden cows, lazy, across
the other side of the low river.

Bare earth on the path is deep-cracked,
no rain for a month,
barely any since February torrents,
when all these meadows were underwater,
the clue, in their name – Water End.

It never rains but it pours,
feast or famine, plague.

Riverside terrace foundations shift and settle,
move with the water table;
it was ever thus,
more so before flood defences.
Jimmy Mack the joiner tells us,

*when I was a lad, these houses flooded
every year* – the houses of The Railway Poor.

And as for the flowers,
like viruses, we name, we classify, we quell.
My Dad could name them all,
but I never listened, more interested
in shops and streets and towns.

And would I like them more if I knew their names:
the ones we give them,

not the names they give themselves.

Dreamcatcher

sometime between Christmas Day and New Year's Eve 2020

A strange gift from a Christian boss,
this dreamcatcher hangs above my bed.

I think of her every time I dust it.

It doesn't always work for the good,
captures dreams I'd rather not remember.

Last night, or somewhere in the early hours,

I dream a January holiday
with an unusual mix of poetry friends

in unsuitable cabins with few mod cons,

no curtains or doors on the ancient showers,
holes in the floor, inadequate heating.

Cabins, like us, that have seen better days.

Although they should be tethered to the ground,
I find myself in the naked shower, being towed to

God-knows-where, by some bloke in a Land Rover.

But, do you know what,
in these constricted times,

      I'd settle for that adventure.

Cemetery Lane

i.m. Barbara Brown & Ann Egglestone

Striding down Abbey Road, back and neck
aching, up past the Juniors to the top of the bank,
crossing the car-heavy B6280,
turning right to follow the familiar track,
rustling through leaves, a remnant of Autumn;

looking over the brick wall into the graveyard,
imagining the stone angel, her wings unfurled,
flying like the winter crow above the beeches;
thinking of Ann, her plaque in the memorial garden;

remembering that confident high school girl
cycling, gabardine open, along Cemetery Lane
pedalling past the lanky grammar school boys,

dashing, sweaty – late again for registration;
visiting Barbara in the stuffy care home,

recalling that careless lazy girl I used to be.

Surrender Bridge

Smelt Mill, Swaledale

before lead   no track
my wild fleck moor
bog   moss   peat
heather shiver in high heat

my tears ran clean
                un-named, unknown
until they came
hell-bent
        picks, hammers, shock, toil
        tore back my skin
        bored deep into my flesh/bone

insect men   down to my veins
dragged out my ore
        their noisy clatter
took their fill
always more   always more

till all was spent

they went
left poisoned spoil
and their names for my streams:
Hard Level Gill, Old Gang Beck

You must come to them sideways

the things you have hidden under the eaves.
This loft is too narrow for straight talking
and although you're up in the roof, you feel
like you're walking through the valley of the shadow.

Like when you glimpse something
                    from the corner of your eye,
and you're not sure if it's really there,
or   if it is   why?

But there's a reason for the hiding.
And if you rummage through the dark hoards
you've squirrelled away all your small life,
you may not/will not like what you find.

And yet, the compulsion is to dig, scratch a scab,
poke a spelk with a rusty needle,
unable to contemplate that you won't be able
to put things right.   Think on –

sometimes it's best to let things lie.

Digging up the Past

i.m. my great grandmother Louisa Smither

(i)
who would've known
         how interest in genealogy
all these years later
         would become an industry
when, in your day
         the aim was to hide your origin
your upbringing
         your sin (if sin
it was) lying
         nudging the facts

how what was shame
         to you, would be fascinating
to your descendants

(ii)
Louisa, Louisa,
you fabricated a father,
configured him as engineer,
lied yourself 2 years younger,
it's all there on your marriage lines.

Netted a hard but respectable husband,
gave birth to 6 legitimate children,
buried one, Maud, as a young woman,
lost your son, Harry, to the Titanic,
hid the illegitimate firstborn.

You did well.
You were gentle, kind,
adored by your grandchildren.
And now someone wants to find out,
rake over the long-cold ashes.

Oh the powerlessness of the long dead poor.

Pit Brow Lasses

Before The Mines and Collieries Act (1842)

We worked down the mines,
yes, and the bairns too, hurriers,
hauling the coal the men hewed
from the rock. My God, it was hot,
unbearable. And, like the fellas,
we stripped to the waist.
No-one seemed to give a toss.

But the trousers we wore
really wound them up. Lord Ashley,
incensed by the hole at the crotch,
by the chain passing high
between our legs... as if
we liked it ourselves, but needs must.

'Any sight more disgustingly indecent,
 revolting,' he said, 'can scarcely
be imagined than these girls at work.
No brothel can beat it.' We laughed
that his nobleness, The Lord,
knew all about brothels.

After The Act

Also known as Tip Girls, Pit Bank Women,
Pit Brow Lasses – we work with the men
as surface labourers. Our 'uniform':
clogs, trousers covered with a skirt
and apron, old flannel jackets
or shawls, and headscarves
to protect our hair
from the bloody dust.

Calls for us to get back in the kitchen.

We lasses, though, are having none of it.
Ridiculous in this day and age – 1887.
The Mayoress of Wigan gives us her blessing:
we twenty-two, in our work togs, march
on parliament to meet the Home Secretary.

We win. Proud to be labelled –
an 'invasion of colliery Amazons'.

The postcards

Arthur Munby, Cambridge prof,
showed more than an interest in us
working in dirty, strange conditions:
paid us lucky 'sitters' a shilling,

to pose with sieves and shovels,
against a woodland backdrop – he said
was worthy of some bloke called Reynolds –
like so many pithead Britannias.

Touched-up tinted photographs,
snapped up as souvenir postcards.
Ah, the fascination of the middle classes
with us pit brow lasses.

The Black Path

always attracted to the dirty path, the post-industrial track now
almost disappeared, but still named;

a painting by Norman Cornish: Durham miners in flat caps, coat
collars turned up against the north-east wind, carrying their bait
and lamps, treading The Black Path: there and back in every
season. There – a day at the seam, underground. Home for a bath
in front of the range in the back-kitchen;

Darlington Black Path, more of a railway track – Faverdale,
Stooperdale, veer past The Whessoe, past where allotments used
to be, to Hopetown and the Working Men's Club: John's Dad
in later years on the door, drinking, the only bone of contention
in a long marriage brokered by Methodism and teetotalism;

what are these contradictory urges: the urge to move beyond, to
climb to high paths, where you meet no-one, and the views are
almost all sky through every shade of blue to charcoal grey;

and the urge to potter in the depths, forgotten, unloved, grubby?

it's the highs and lows, the ethereal and the raunchy,
the state of blessedness, the state of sin.

Echoes

                    All I remember:
tin bath in front of the fire in the back kitchen,
wooden-seated outside lav, being incarcerated
in the front bedroom with scarletina,
so the new baby – I loathed him – didn't catch it;
        Wrexham. I recognise nothing of the town:
our house in Smithfield Road, brewery chimney,
and the tomb of Elihu Yale, benefactor of that
famous university. I might have found familiar
the Salvation Army Hall, but they knocked it down,
replaced it with something modern, bland.
                    I still have vivid horrors of the 1950's
hospital ward: I am 2 with poorly ears. Mum peeping
through the glass-paned doors, they won't let her in,
might upset me, and crying for two abandoned weeks.
I think they hit me.
                    But I knew nothing of the mines and
Gresford Colliery Explosion – 2 o'clock in the morning:
266 killed, 6 saved, 11 bodies recovered;
                                    that the mine owners
docked half a day's pay. After all, the men worked only
half a shift.

Dinosaurs

after Robert Desnos

We lived in those times of grants and fees paid
we ordinary girls from poor backgrounds;
post-war optimism, the baby-boomers;
we National-Healthy girls who went
to new and red-brick universities,
each outnumbered five to one by men.
                    And we weren't grateful.
And lots of us made our own clothes:
psychedelic mini-skirts, velvet loons.

We lived in those times of student revolution.
A girl on our corridor hanged herself one morning –
after her year in France, the Paris riots –
while we were *sitting in* The Great Hall,
storming the Administration, colonising
the Vice-Chancellor's office – that time of
free discos, walks back to digs at daybreak,
threats that we'd all be sent down.

How lucky we were and we didn't know it,
plenty of jobs, cheap flats, no loans, no debt
to hang round our middle-aged necks.
We dinosaurs.

At 29

for Tom

he's not averse to their bunions, hard skin,
although he keeps his own hammer toes
a secret, locked away in staff-discounted
Barkers, Cheaneys or Ted Bakers; he loves
the artistry of double-stitching, leather soles,
the touch of green or heather tweed
in the up-market deep-tan brogues;

and he's proud of his ability to sell,
to share his passion, chat to find
a customer's weakness, discuss
the smell of good hide, the shoemaker's
attention to detail, fine laces; he knows
his trade and relishes an orderly stockroom:
keeps note of what has sold well,
what must be reduced; he's good at this

but he hates the long hours, shoe-horn pay,
three flights of stairs, the feckless manager,
his titanic debt with Student Loans. And
worst of all, his lack of status and a certain
cultural attitude towards those who serve.

Autumn

My landscape has changed in this dying season –
last flourish before everything turns bleak;
cold enough to wear my rough Icelandic jumper
but not cold enough for hat and scarf and gloves.

We don't do dark-haired Winter babies,
all Taurus, Gemini, Cancer, Leo,
but here you are, born at the end of Libra,
to weigh us in your scales: balance our waning,

jolt us out of long-locked waiting.   Alba, sunrise,
hard to avoid the clichés, you take me by surprise,
bring me something I was needing, give me a word
I've been in the habit of avoiding: joy.

Twins

For Oliver

13 January 2022

Your birth – I wasn't there
I only have reportage.
You came in camouflage,
firstborn of twins –
identical.

For Joseph

Tiny person
        we met you
                for a little while
minute perfection
          in your crystal cave
                    enshrined in love
how glad we were
        to greet you
            wish you could have stayed
a moment longer
        but thank you
           for the time you came to bless our lives.

(ii) *17 January 2022*

Not for you an undramatic exit:
nestled in your mother's arms

you took your leave,
Wolf Moon huge in January sky.

Now we are left to grieve.

Snow Moon

We drive home over Stainmore,
a month to the day, Joseph,
that we said goodbye

and we drove the same route
under the magical light
of Wolf Moon rising.

This time, Snow Moon appears,
pops up above the hills,
orange, huge,

such a shock in the dark,
I almost leave the road
from staring.

The temperature's dropping,
enough to trigger gritting
as we listen

to red warnings of Storm Eunice –
tomorrow she'll come.
But Oliver,

this is your event,
your second full moon,
and today,

you are five weeks old
and we have been allowed
to see you again,

touch your lovely warm
and perfect skin.
Can such a tiny person

know his own mind, play up,
show disapproval?
What we see

and what we know, Oliver,
is that you have you own forms
of communication.

We take note.

Moon Baby

I measure your progress in moons,
Oliver, miracle baby, born
at 22 weeks: 400 grams.

You weren't expected to survive.
Your twin brother Joseph didn't.
He died at four days old,

when Wolf Moon was full.
But you
snuck in, hung on,

keeping a low profile:
no expectation, no expectation.
You had the moon

in your sights, weathered
Snow Moon, Worm Moon,
holding on for Easter:

first Sunday after the full moon
after the vernal equinox.
I used to teach this,

had a sort of quiz,
a formula for kids
who finished all their work,

to calculate the date
for as many years
as it took the bell to ring.

And you're still here – Pink Moon,
a resurrection. A triumph
of medical science

and I don't devalue that,
but you are a magic baby,
more than a miracle of nature.

Blood Moon

Lunar Eclipse

I missed it. Hardly surprising.

4 a.m. Heavy snoring.
And thick cloud covering
for those awake
who hoped to see it.

The garden is awash
with pink and lilac,
and today we celebrate
your official birth date.

You were never planned
to be a Winter baby,
a child of late Spring
who couldn't wait.

But you've made it through
to another full moon
and soon, you can see the world
outside a hospital ward.

And what a time you'll have.

Weight

Not quite a pound of sugar
you carried no weight of expectation
just a whisper of 'maybe'
but 'probably not'.

The weight of evidence
came down on 5% to zero
so the flutter of 'possibly'
like an imperceptible wisp of voile
fell still as we held our breath
and waited
minute by minute
hour by hour
day by night and day
month after month
each with its new jolt of heavy fear
at every monitor bleep, the wavy lines
as you swing from OK to dangerous.

And as you grow, gain weight,
although we know, and say,
'Not out of the woods yet'
the harder it is to measure
the weight of our hope.

Due Date

Surviving twin,
identical brother:

he has his mother's chin,
his father's toes,

and if you catch him
in a certain pose,

he has his Grandma's nose,
poor speck. And when

we look at him,
we see the other.

Home

We drive through biblical rain,
a second baptism:
your first, at 3 days old,

the hospital chaplain
saving you from limbo –
but you didn't go.

And so,
today we fetch you home,
tiny as a tiny newborn.

And at last,
we get to see you in the flesh,
hold you.

Reflections

It catches you,
not at that moment –
paddling for the first time
on Scarborough sands
with your tiny son,
walking behind him
holding one of his hands held high,
his other arm outstretched for balance;
full of delight: his and yours,
at new sensations –

but later,
studying the photograph
captured on his mother's phone,
seeing the other – mirror image
reflected in the water – imagining,
remembering his twin brother.

Without darkness – no stars

From light into darkness
                            she climbs the stairs
arrives, like Concorde
                            on the edge of space

What is she thinking
                            let me guess
Where is she taking us
                            we couldn't care less
Shall we take sandwiches
                            maybe, yes.

The Bungalow of the Seven Veils

for Jackie

The first veil is cast off from my eyes
as the train sails past my destination;
I should have read the departure board
at Darlington Railway Station.

> *and the train guard might have told me*
> *it didn't stop at Durham.*

The second, as I experience the arsines
of the porter at Newcastle, and third,
the helpfulness of the taxi driver
who gets me to the hard-to-find cul-de-sac in time.

> *is it worth the wait – a nice enough outlook*
> *for a 50s box with UPVC double glazing?*

Fourth veil, Jackie and the estate agent
take me into the two bedrooms with grim
built-in wardrobes and the smell of plug-in
air fresheners trying to hide the damp.

> *better I think to save your money on those*
> *they never work, indicate trouble.*

Fifth, we need to see past the decor,
kitchen very pine and a good size, a pantry,
lots of cupboards. A useful ladder reveals
the sixth – a possible loft conversion.

> *a third bedroom, and this will add value;*
> *dreams of a library in the eaves.*

But nothing prepares me for the seventh,
why we are here, the true revelation,
uninterrupted view from the sitting room windows:
huge sky, late Spring tree tops,

> *Flass Vale in all her naked glory.*

Ladies on a Terrace with Sparklers

from an image in the British Museum, Moghul India 1730–1740

for Alice and Frances

We met on the terrace
        stood   facing each other
                        unable to touch

kept apart by tradition,
        by culture, religion,
                the ornamental pond.

She was so gorgeous,
        her fine chiffon long skirt
                the opposite of modest,

revealing her long legs
                her pantalooned thighs.
                        She wore a gold turban

with bird of paradise feathers,
                her untamed raven hair fell free
                        down her back in waves.

Behind us,
        the ink-black sky, lit up
                by dots of stars

by golden fireworks
                like regiments of eagles.
                        We couldn't disguise

the frisson between us
        could not take our eyes off each other,
                        the electric gap bridged

by the sparklers we raised
        towards one another
                        across the divide.

        The sparks flew and kissed.

The love was explosive
        unspoken
                and it changed us forever.

We could never go back.

Washing her Trousers

for Helen

She has bought fish for me,
rare fish caught from the overfished
North Sea, it drips on her clothes:
her purple T shirt, her brown cords,
infusing a slow-releasing scent.

We put up with it for hours.
Then she peels off both
plunges them into a deep suds bowl.

The trousers exhale
a cornucopia of smells, first fish,
then their aromatic ancestry:

cotton pods   pickers' sweat
man-made dye

freight-container hold
sea fret in their folds

fusty warehouse   diesel lorry
chain-store hint

pristine office   charitybag
backroom mould

Fairy   Comfort   steam   febreze
for second-hand rose

arnica   dampdog   ambergris
allotment   garden   fennel   mint

mud in her turn-ups
honeysuckle on her thighs.

Choosing an Animal to Bring You Back

i.m. Joanna Boulter, died 13 September 2019

So, how to find an animal to bring you back:
acerbic, generous, funny, fierce,
never afraid to make a sharp remark,
contrary, holding me in your unblinking stare.

Not lithe, nor fast enough to be a hare,
no boxing mating ritual; I never saw
you dance, although I didn't know you
in your courting days. You never ran,
didn't see the point of walking for fun.

You chose a rabbit as your alter ego. Why?
Not fluffy, cuddly or cute, perhaps you liked
the startled look, the raising of the head,
turning from side to side, alert to danger,
then scampering for the safety of the burrow.

Wise owl, what was it like when you began
to lose your mind, lost the physical ability
to write? When you took to your nest,
and stayed until the cancer killed you?

And when you stopped all medication,
what was it like when you rode the first
wild horses of returning reason, how
the poetry came back, how you found
the energy to finalise your last collection?

No, I choose a herring gull in profile:
acute ear – never tin; your fixing eye
menaces, until you laugh and your face
softens. Always the possibility of flight,
of freedom, how you soared
above the body's tethering.

night on the ocean

fog   mist   an echo   a watery moon
night on the ocean

our boat is adrift (is our boat adrift?)

someone is calling through a muffled megaphone –
who knows what they are saying?

waves slap against the prow
as we plough through the depths

our boat is not adrift
we are adrift
this barque knows where it is going

maybe someone is in charge
but they won't tell us

or if they do   it will be through a muffled megaphone

ocean   night   a watery moon
an echo   mist   fog
adrift

The Whitby Bull

The sound of my 20s: The Whitby Bull
booming through deadened air.

I taught Yvonne;
   she often looked exhausted,
lived in the house beneath the foghorn,
her dad, the keeper of the light.
       The Bull
was loud for us, deafening for her.
Every other noise was muffled,
like the sound equivalent of blackout
in The War.
       The Fret
folded itself round us like a damp duvet,
strangled us like a wayward sheet,
as we wrestled our way to *The Plough*
on November nights, past the spectral
forms of trawlers in the harbour,
street lights dimmed.
     But August was worse,
the rest of the country swimming
in summer heat while we shivered
in shorts under cold wadding, the sun,
a pale powerless glint beyond our reach.
       Disappointed
families from boiling cities,
out for a day on the beach, clutched
buckets and spades and candy floss,
trying, as we do, to make the best of it.

The Bull has gone, so have those trawlers,
but The Fret remains. Constant.

Sound Bank

He mentions how he loves to walk
under an umbrella in the rain, how its drumming
gives him so much pleasure; he doesn't get the irony –
how much she yearns for this, and the beating
of a downpour on her night-time window pane.
The bloody useless fusing of the tiny bones
in her middle ear: malleus, incus, stapes.

Tomorrow: she'll walk along the water's edge
towards the mouth of the German blockhaus,
imagine the bay they watched in the war,
catalogue her vision, plunder her sound bank
to recall waves shushing on the shore, racket
of children shrieking, splashing, the *pock pock*
of that couple with bat and ball. Remember,

and record it all.

On Removing Her Hearing Aids

In my night time silent world
I hear the history of my home

the scratch of Saxon burial
and rattle of passing cart.

Then later, the whistle, slap
and tap of Blackett's builders.

Is that the maid-of-all-work
whispering her prayers,

and in the still-dark morning, cleaning
out grates, clattering the coals?

Can I make out the whine and bark
of a procession of poorly dogs,

mewing sick cats, rustling pet rodents
brought for succour to a previous owner?

And could that be the wireless broadcasting
the outbreak of the Second World War

or something more recent,
something much more scary?

Still (Life)

Before we lived here
                    even before
the Saxon cemetery
                    when this place
was simply a river valley
                     the steep banks down into town
and up to the railway station
                    were the wild banks of the Skerne
before the river was named
                    with its wetlands, trees and scrub
and no people
                    what creatures lived here
before we concreted it over
                    corralled small sections
called it our own?

So why am I surprised
                    when I go out at night
after heavy rain in August
                    into my back yard
trigger the security light
                    to stumble upon a fat still toad
a pulse in its throat
                    watching
a damp-loving snail
                    both waiting for me
to go back inside
                    trigger the dark
leave them to complete
                    their last transaction.

The Maid's Room

i.m. Sarah Crowhurst

Five bedrooms, and hers,
the only one with no fireplace.
And an air-vent to make sure
she's not too cosy.

Her room faces due east
and on fine mornings, the sun
shines straight in, not that she
can spend much time there.

Maid of all work
she would've been called,
like my granny at just seventeen
up at all hours, alone
with the Home Counties' gentleman
she kept house for.

The Hole

There were two, but one got broken
years ago, plastic seahorses
in aqua tinged with gold,
bathroom ephemera, doomed to drown.

One Christmas day in a rage
she ripped off all the barely hanging
wallpaper although the single seahorse
remained like a blot.

Today, when she was dusting
she dislodged the reminder;
it fell into the roll-top bath,
shattered – an accident.

She thought she'd hang
something else on the accusing nail,
something tiny, something seasidey,
but cursory searching offered no replacement,

so taking the pliers from her husband's study
she carefully pulled the nail out –
not too painful, satisfying in fact
to see the small hole, like some act

of sympathetic magic.

The Lock

Two keyholes,
both with brass escutcheons,

the younger at eye height,
the older at hand.

The original worked a treat,
until it didn't.

'Oil is what it needs,' I thought,
gave it a good dose of *3 in 1.*

We had to call the locksmith in.
'These rare locks have complex mechanisms.

The worst thing you can do
is oil them.'

The new lock meets all insurance specifications,
but I loathe its brassy cover,

not soft golden
like its obsolete elder brother.

When we come home tired, maybe after
a long day out, a short break, a drink or two,

unthinking,
the key always finds its way to the old familiar

and it cannot let us in.

Refuge

Always my room; still lock it every night
although I leave the key. Now anyone can go in.
And I don't mind now. There are other empty rooms.

> But when there were kids who lived at home,
> it was *Mum's Room*, where she went to work –
> she said – early evening, as the sun set into
> the lightest room in a light Edwardian house.

Although it's in a landlocked town, my room
favours the sea; all shades of blue and grey
and turquoise. And seagrass carpet like sand.

> Such a busy life, she needed an excuse –
> a place to be on her own, to listen to *U2*, join in:
> 'I gave you everything you wanted'. She knows
> there has to be more. She plans, hatches, yearns.

Her room – still a place to dream, imagine,
recall when she lived by the coast; she thinks
she will again, but for now, she'll stay put.

No Sanctuary

She's moved her desk in,
       says she won't intrude.
It's changed the ambience,
       the mood.
She's brought a filing cabinet, pens,
       a wire tray for bills,
keeps opening and closing drawers,
       snapping shut a ring binder,
whispering or humming to herself.

Sometimes, she tidies up a bit,
       hoovers the ancient rugs,
tuts at the clouds of dust she raises,
       glittering in full sun,
runs her forefinger across the windowpane,
       cleans it with *Windolene*.

I can't play my jazz CDs when she's there
       or listen to Radio 3.
She doesn't come in much, for long,
       but she 'pops' in,
interrupts.
       I have a door with a lock,
a sign to hang on the knob, '*caution,*
       artist at work',
which she ignores.

Moon Landing, Barron Street

The night the first man landed on the moon,
quiet John, at number 61, was watching it on the telly.

Mrs Smith, at 59, got the police round,
'That lad next door, he's been out on the street singing –

such a racket, enough to fetch the houses down,
swinging from the lamp posts, carrying on.

Some nights, he tries to break in, come through the wall.
I've piled up all these old biscuit tins to keep him out.

That lad, nowt but trouble, with his black velvet jacket
and wild, long hair. Sometimes, he brandishes a flute,

keeps a mouth organ up his sleeve, goes to that den
of iniquity, that art college in the Boro.'

She asked me round once – so she could toast
the wayward lad's bride – gave me a half of Advocaat,

when I asked for a lemonade. I wonder if the aspidistra
survived? Mad as a snake, like Mrs Moore over the road,

who said her husband was very plastic.

Walls Pie Factory, Hyde

That time after Hindley but before Shipman,
early morning briskwalk to Stalybridge station
for the train to Hyde – blackened chimneys,
silent brick walls, erstwhile clogs clattering
on cobbles – we clock-on at 7.30 sharp,
our wages docked for every minute late.

This was in the days of August Wakes Weeks,
most of the workforce off to Blackpool
we students employed to fill the gap –
our promise to work the full vacation.
In need of money, I missed my last family holiday
but many broke faith, left anyway.

Useless on piece-work, annoying the nimble,
I dropped more party pies than I could pack –
was demoted to something messier, something
slower, to fashion large sausage meat balls,
plunging my hands into massive pink vats
containing everything but the whistle.

The hottest summer for ages – we toiled at huge
move-thru ovens that spat out mince and steak & kidney –
iced lime juice dispensed from galvanised buckets,
at irregular intervals, in tiny card cones,
as we tapped the pies out of their tins,
burning our hands in a baptism of hot gravy.

Winterings

The fields quivering, the skyline a grimace

more like a rictus sneer
as if there's evil in the air,
something to make your hair stand up,
something of deep pain,
something of death.

Oblivious,
in the long-abandoned farmhouse –
hunkering in the lee of limestone cliffs –
our couple kiss: a beginning.
Who knows where it will end?

Winterings Again

And the air was full of something
and I wanted to stay put, inside:

familiarity of the moth-eaten armchair,
dirty flagstone floor, the knackered range,
once, I guess, a pristine, warm farm kitchen.

They would go out, down to the pub,
The Kings Head – vertical descent
to the beck, then a mile of stony scrabbling.

I was pleased and scared to be alone,
a lot of changes rattling inside my skull.

Outside – the flashes and spells of wizard light
dance and leap across the top of the fells.

And then, maybe lost, maybe sheltering,
a large black and white cow lumbers in, as shocked
as I am by the storm, her unexpected presence.

I'm no herdsman, but breathless, I shush her out.
Settled again when they burst in, every hair
on their heads standing upright.

They didn't make it to the pub.
As I said, the air was full of something.

From a Distance

Battleship grey, like your eyes,
my new lover says; I discover
he's rarely any good with colour;

the North Sea is never turquoise
but today, it's turning even darker,
more like thunderstorm,

verging on indigo.   I long to be
back in the Golfe du Morbihan,
in its small bays' translucent water,

feel the tiny fish nibbling around
my toes, before I take a deep breath
and dive in.   From Ty Bihan beach,

the sea is sparkling, shimmering, calm,
that ice-pure blue of Scandinavian skies.
From the sea, the dull sand is golden.

A Doctor's Questions

Tell me, Mrs Foster, what does the barometer read today?
How do the clouds look? Are they lowering?

Can you feel any dampness in the air?
Should I take my good coat?

Did you notice if the large hole in the track has been filled in?
What do you mean the farrier couldn't shoe Dobbin?

Why did we move to the country?
Why did we believe the estate agent

when he said it was only a stone's throw from Gloucester?
How far can an estate agent throw a stone?

Where did you put my sturdy boots?
Have you packed my lancing tools and laudanum?

How can I tell if I'll be back for dinner?

Kink

The image on my mobile phone,
North Sea, Sheringham – a summer sunset:
pebble beach, wooden groynes,

the sun, just sinking at that mid point
causing a bright kink in the straight line
where sky meets sea. It makes me smile.

At least it did.
        Now it spells trouble on the horizon.
Impending gloom.

Today at ophthalmology, I see the scan,
a bright kink on the retina of my left eye –
the macula, a tiny spot that governs vision.

Nothing to worry about the eye doctor says,
except six months ago it wasn't there. Good news,
my right eye shows no sign of getting worse.

               Live with it.
We only do the operation if it causes bother,
provokes distortion, or letters start to disappear.

They promise to keep an eye on it.
He'd sign me off, if this second eye
hadn't decided to join in with the other –

envy, desire for its own epiretinal membrane –
and also because he sees I'm terrified
of going blind as well as deaf.

He chats amiably,
says how after the age of 35, something
goes wrong every five years.

I calculate, that's two things for him
and six for me. I make a mental list –
he's right I think.

C/Old

You can set your clock by it:

postprandial, settling down to watch TV.
I've lit the fire: its satisfying crackle and spit,
corralled behind a sturdy iron guard,
suggests a sense of life, of wildness
rendered safe, reducing heat to warmth.

That nothing hour between the news and
Scandi noir, a time to have a cup of tea, to flick
through Catch-up: unmissable programmes
that I've missed; some worthy things I feel
I ought to watch, or comedies that leave me

cold. I'll try this five-star documentary –
latest discoveries at Stonehenge. The tea
arrives. I take a sip, tune in my hearing aids
to the loop – it's magical: perfect sound
beamed to the vacant gap between my ears.

I really try to concentrate on this bearded bloke
in muddy shorts, shouting through mist
about some bit of pot or flint-knapped stone.
I start to drift.   The observer says I nod
my head, or throw it back, begin to snore,

until the final credits roll. I snort, come to,
take another sip of tea. It's cold.

The Cartoonist

Always a pen or a pencil.
No, not quite right.

Even with no pen or paper
the same gesture
imaginary *Rapidograph*
held in his left hand
between thumb and forefinger
scribbling on the dining room table.

Always, as a child, before
he could speak, his Mam told me,
'No bother – give him some
pencils and paper;
he would draw for hours.'

And when he was older,
to flatten them, he put his paintings
under the living room carpet –
his sisters in their stilettos
pinpricked them all.
He wasn't deterred.

Now, in the corner of the room
in his new, deep red winged chair,
tiny spiral-bound sketchbook
on his lap, black inkpen drooping
in his slackening grasp, his head
starts to nod, fall forward.

And she, mindful of previous disasters:
paint splashes on walls, ink stains
on carpets, is more concerned
to protect the gorgeous fabric
than to worry about his exhaustion.

She cannot let him sleep
until he has replaced his pen top,
put his ideas to one side.

The Big Skirt

after 'Mrs Degas Vacuums the Floor' by Sally Swain

Monday morning and I should be cleaning.
Instead I'm sitting in a Herefordshire mansion
laughing, eating and writing this.

The Artist is at home, hundreds of miles away.
I wonder if he's sticking to the schedule –
it's the turn of the dining room and kitchen.

I bet he's skiving seeing I'm not there
to crack the whip   maybe he's sloped off
to our local *Strictly Come Dancing Academy.*

He's not bothered about the slinky Cha Cha Cha
or the hot Tango. He likes voluminous frocks,
dancers with a multitude of net petticoats.

I thought perhaps I could keep his interest,
popped down to *Oxfam*, got a big checked skirt,
almost floor length, with racy buttons

from hem to thigh, that pop open when I stretch
with the feather duster, when I kneel to scrub
the floor, when I vacuum the stairs.

It looks more than fetching with my big pink
spotty slippers and sage fleece cardigan.
But, when we pause for morning coffee, the talk

is of *Hoover* bags and *Mr Muscle* bathroom wipes
and lavatory cleaner,   of test match scores and
questions about what we'll have for dinner.

Goo goo g'joob

Le Massina bar, Rond-point De Gaulle,
Plouharnel Friday Market

The egg man isn't here today.
Maybe his hens aren't laying.
Last week, he drove his van

into the pavement parasols,
oblivious of we old hippies
lapping up September sun.

The bloody traffic's here though
on this main route to Quiberon:
huge lorries of every kind,

multitudes of campervans, and
surfers, off to the Côte Sauvage
pour Le Weekend. The convoy

of Bikers, all the same, all
desperate to be different,
younger.   Over fifty years,

we reminisce, since John sang
I am the walrus, admire
the ancient cyclist, posing

in Piet Mondrian windcheater
and vibrant yellow baseball cap
Not dead yet. No, not dead yet.

At 72

Plage de Saint-Colomban

Emerging from the sea
in her gaudy tankini –
styled for the fuller figure
by M&S –

she reflects,

she ain't no Ursula Andress.
To be frank, she never was,

although, once,
there may have been
a flicker of interest
from two young men on the water's edge,

but now, nothing,
not even a snigger.

After the Bunion Op

Discovering ourselves in a strange and cheap housing estate
                                        near the sea –
the 60's concrete school, at first sight, single storey
with a swimming pool on the flat roof,
but on experiencing it, a building with many layers
and impenetrable;
                        trying to find our way round,
we keep asking helpful-looking people on various
                                                Help Desks,
realising, at last, we would never get out,
recognising a barbecued foot on the banqueting table,
slow horror dawning.
                        How did we end up here?
Was it the Chinese grave armour in Durham's Oriental
                                                Museum –
carved jade feet and shin pads lying in the locked cabinet,
perfect straight toes pointing heavenwards?
Or could it have been that massive stone foot (Roman?)
in the statue hall at Chatsworth?

Ghentish Town

Stuck in the Impasse of the who-knows-what,
a train to catch, just tell yourself, without
conviction, *the race is not to the swift*.
Though you speak no Flemish, you'll
have to ask this passer-by for directions.

She squawks something about a bar,
called *Seven Stars*, signs left, right, left.
She tries but *wastes her time* and mine.
Face it girl, you're lost again. Another
monumental mockery, you *take the instant
way* into *the early afternoon shadows*.

Ghent

On the day we are due to leave,
'Plenty of time', I say, 'between

checking out and our train's departure.
Plenty of time for a little adventure.'

History (I never learn) is peppered with
getting lost. And I have total confidence:

in my faulty compass, my faulty clock.

John has learned not to disagree,
is complicit in my self-deception.

He tags along as we walk, stride,
almost-run, further and further

into the working-class labyrinth
of Ghent's outskirts – nothing medieval,

picturesque, or quaint.   Stuck
and time is running out. We speak

no Flemish, the populace, no English.

At last, a kind woman does her best
in guttural tones with frantic gestures.

And we get something of the picture,
head off, thankfully, towards the station:

too fast, too sweaty, too old in fact,
old enough to know

Trapped

after Magritte

I managed it once,
           saw myself in my wife's glass:
a dull man in a black bowler hat
looked out from the silver sand;
he had gold in his hand.

I quit my job,
           tossed my hat into the sea,
bought my wife some satin ribbon;
she fashioned a bow, pinned it
in her greying hair.

In her last days,
           she ate like a bird,
pecked at her food,
left her teeth in the russet apple
she'd requested.

I lit a candle in her memory,
           but it sheds no light.
And every night,

when I lay down to sleep,
           she haunts me,
wraps me in her bloody shroud,
makes me lie in that cheap wood box
I laid her in.

How you carry on in *the banality of things*

even when the deck is listing from starboard to port,
how you keep putting one foot in front of the other,
swaying from side to side,
just about managing to maintain your balance;

how your boat stays afloat
while you work out how to sink the locked box,
send it to the bottom of the deepest of the deep,
secured with triple locks that won't rust in brine;

but you're haunted by Pandora,
how it all spills out, just at that moment
when you're thinking about nothing in particular,
sitting in your comfortable place in warm sun,

contemplating the ocean, the horizon, sipping
strong coffee; perhaps it's a smell, the trigger –
like the smell of oiled rope in the museum –
that unmistakeable stench of loathing, fear, shame;

how it all comes back in dreams,
and how there's no control of the subconscious,
like trying to stay upright on this rocking boat,
like trying to hold back the tide.

On teaching myself not to listen

Long hard benches in the Citadel,
military ranks facing the officer
and the Penitent Form.
                        Unforgiving wood
for tender bums and knobbly knees
as we prayed on bare floorboards.
Knee Drill my Dad called
                        the prayer meeting.
How to disappear into imagination,
sideline the smells of mansion polish,
that animal glue that had to be melted
in an old tin on the coke stove
                                to paste up
salvation posters. Do I remember
undeodorised armpits, bodies that bathed
once a week at the most?
                        I'm not sure.
How to ignore the holy missives
painted on walls, on the Mercy Seat,
'God First', other texts I can't recall;
block out the appeals, the choruses –
Out from his wounded side...
Though your sins be as scarlet... –
the testimonies, 'if he could love a sinner
like me...'
                And how to escape into laughter
as I got older, double entendres
in the songs, dirty bits in the Bible,
catching a glimpse of Mum's bloomers
as she sat on the platform, and tried
to look like she was paying attention
to Dad's sermon, giggling

as she tuned her hearing aid
into the radio of the fish & chip shop
next door.
            In that interminable boredom,
a childhood of meetings, I practised the art
of not listening. I learnt my lesson well.

Being Gemini

Vanitas Vanitates et Omnia Vanitas

                They knew a thing or two
those 18th century modellers and carvers,

about the transience of life, the futility
of pleasure, the certainty of death.

Like that Eliot poem about Webster,
the skull beneath the skin,

this wax Vanitas head haunts me,
with its half-and-half image:

red lips, golden curls, jewelled bracelet,
a living hand holding a posy of fading flowers;

the skull, a skeletal claw, snake,
spider, snail, maggots.

Fading is the worldling's pleasure
I sang as a child.

                But I'm always Gemini,
whatever my puritan upbringing tells me:

the falseness of horoscopes, the wickedness of magic,
the dangerous paths that are not the true path;

about the great aunt, mentioned now and then,
who lived somewhere near Tunbridge Wells.

They muttered she could make warts disappear.
And there are some things you just know.

And it takes a bit of a shock to own up to them,
the shock of the lump growing for god-knows-how-long,

long enough to be big enough to cause trouble
and not benign enough to leave alone.

And then, on top of that, there's this pandemic,
bringing us face to face with our own mortality.

So here I am, as ever,   split down the middle,
neither one thing nor   the other. Being Gemini.

Notes

MCC learns a lesson from cricket

I was named Marilyn Carol Crowhurst so that my cricket-mad Dad and elder brother could refer to me as MCC. Cricket aficionados will understand this. We had a large urn-like sugar bowl which we called The Ashes. Another cricket fan, whenever he came to tea, took pleasure in returning The Ashes to the MCC.

Landlocked Ramble

The end words of each line are taken from the Robert Frost quotation.

You must come to them sideways

Title from *Mirrors at 4 a.m.* by Charles Simic

Pit Brow Lasses

After The1842 Mines and Collieries Act, most women were replaced with more expensive pit ponies. Some women did surface work at the coal screens on the pit bank (or brow): emptying coal tubs, sorting coal and picking out stones, and shifting it on to wagons. The last pit brow lass retired in the 1970s. This poem came from a project by Vane Women, writing in response to *Breaking Ground – Women of the Northern Coalfields* at The Mining Art Gallery, Bishop Auckland, an exhibition celebrating 100 years since some women first got the vote.

Echoes

The miners' hymn, *Gresford*, written in 1936 by Robert Saint, Hebburn miner and bandsman, is played every year in Durham at The Big Meeting.

Dinosaurs
I lived in those times from *Epitaph* by Robert Desnos

Twins
For Oliver and in memory of Joseph, my identical twin grandsons, born at 22 weeks 3 days in Royal Preston Hospital intensive care neonatal unit January 13th 2022; with love and thanks.

Winterings
Epigraph from *Wind* by Ted Hughes

The Big Skirt
With thanks to the late Penny Minney who organised our stay in the 'Herefordshire mansion'

Ghentish Town
With thanks to lines/ideas from:
Ecclesiastes 9, *Song*, Sir Edmund Waller, *Troilus & Cressida* Act 3: Sc 3, Shakespeare, *As I Walked Out One Evening*, WH Auden, *Gloria mundi est*, Anon

'the banality of things'
This comes from *The Ships of Theseus* by Steve Gehrke

Acknowledgements

With thanks to: Hospitalfield for a two-week residency which gave me time and space to put this collection together, and to Fiona Crangle (fellow resident) for permission to use her paintings on the cover; to Pat Maycroft for working on the front cover design; to MR Peacocke, SJ Litherland and Dorothy Long for help with the manuscript and proof reading. With special thanks to Vane Women and Hallgarth poets who were the first to hear many of these poems.

The *Cluff* cartoon was first published in *The Spectator*.

Thanks to the editors of the following magazines, websites and anthologies where some of these poems have appeared: *Algebra of Owls, Animals, Bakings, Beyond the Storm, Blue Oranges, Bread and Roses, Burn and Rave, Celebration, Dreich, Duo, Ekphrastic, Envoi, New Contexts, The North, Poetry News, Tabula Rasa, Write out Loud* and *What Meets the Eye: Deaf Perspective, Write where we are now* and *Writers' Cafe magazine.*

Trapped was long-listed in the 2023 National Poetry Competition; *Landlocked Ramble* won the 2022 Bowes Museum Regeneration Competition and was displayed in the exhibition; *Moon Baby* was second in the 2022 Ripon Poetry Competition; *Dinosaurs* won the 2016 Holland Park Poetry and Politics competition; *Without darkness – no stars* was commended in the 2015 Poetry Society Stanza Competition; *Dreamcatcher* is performed in British Sign Language by Mary-Jayne Russell de Clifford for Arachne Press (Youtube).